Yes, GOD Is Real

Stories That Speaks His Existence

Toni Henderson-Mayers

word therapy
P U B L I S H I N G

Published by Word Therapy Publishing
July 31, 2018

ISBN-13: 978-0975516379

ISBN-10: 097551637X

Printed in the United States of America all rights reserved under international Copyright laws.

Cover Design by: www.tiffanythebrand.com

Word Therapy Publishing
P.O. Box 939
Hope Mills, NC 28348

www.wordtherapypublishing.com

Dedication

I dedicate this book to you, GOD. I love you. You have been there for me in tough times and when I soared further and higher than I thought possible. You alone were responsible for my existence, my talents, gifts and abilities. You provided a peaceful life and overstocked it with everything I will ever need. When all others turned their back on me, you were right there and when I had nowhere to turn, you took me in. I don't know what I would do without you. Since I was a child I felt your love surround me and you haven't left me as I age and grow older.

To show my love and gratitude, I dedicate this book to you and ask that you allow it to bless others and draw them closer to you. As you enlarge my territory stay with

me and show me how to represent
you well.

Acknowledgements

Thank you to GOD for implanting this idea into my heart, to my husband Brian for his quiet support, my sons Sean and Christian for inspiring me every day, my Mom and Dad for raising me and instilling an awareness of GOD into my life and who model what having a relationship with him is all about and to all of the contributing writers who helped make this book a reality. A special thanks belongs to Tiffany Green for the cover design. See my copyright page for her information.

Table of contents

Introduction

By Toni Henderson-Mayers, MA, MA, MBA

We breathe in and out. A cool breeze rushes over us on a sunny day. Leaves rustle pass our feet as we walk a quiet nature trail. In all these day to day interactions with the air, we never stop and ask if the air we breathe, the cool breeze we experience or the force behind the rustling of the leaves is real. We KNOW the air is real. Yet, we ask at every turn, is God real?

We say we can't see him so therefore God isn't real. We can't see the air, so how do we know it exists? Like the air, God moves in most cases unnoticed. There are times if you focus and pay attention you can trace Him moving in your life. Just as subtle as the air, He moves.

There are times, like the air He moves loudly, dramatically, like a tornado. A tornado, commands respect not because it asks for it, but because IT IS! God is! When God moves in this way, all the earth, the universe knows He is God. Demons quake, angels bow and all of creation worship at His feet. He is God and Yes, He is real!

Every few years, scientists discover an animal in the bottom of the sea, or a molecule or germ they haven't known before. We except they exist without question. In school, I was taught the deeper one went into the ocean, the more exotic the fish became. I was also told that there were animals so deep in the ocean, scientist didn't have a name for them. In addition,

I took a trip when I was a preteen to the Badlands in South Dakota. There was a sign posted just before I went in that stated we would be entering at our own risk. We were taking a risk because the Badlands had animals within it that no man had a name for, knew whether they were harmless or if they even existed. Why did I mention all of this? Is it possible that something can exist without our knowledge? Hmmm!? Thanks something to think about.

Typically, humans can be selfish. The world revolves around us. We are center stage. Only the curious look beyond themselves and the faithful find answers to what they seek. Isaiah 55: 6 (NIV) teaches us to "Seek the Lord while he may be found; call on him while he is near." Just like the air, God leaves evidence of His existence all around us. Sometimes He is subtle and sometimes He is loud, powerful, commanding our respect. Whatever way He shows himself, He is ever present and can be found if we look for Him. The above scripture from the Bible suggest that God is near now, but at some point may withdraw from us. Just like the air, we utilize it every day, not realizing it is a privilege and not a right. Knowing God is a privilege. He wants us to know Him and to develop a relationship with Him. He wants us to call on Him so He can show us the best way to live our lives. He wants to hear our concerns because He has the answer to every problem we may have.

This book, "Yes, God Is Real" is my tribute to God because I KNOW He is real. He has made himself real in my life in so many ways. Of course, I will share my story later in this book, but I wanted others who have experienced God for themselves to contribute as well.

It is my prayer as you read this book, that your faith in God will be renewed or if you are aware of Him for the first time that you will come to know Him in a deep and lasting way. I pray with each turn of the page you will be empowered, encouraged and educated and can say without any hesitation that, "Yes, GOD Is Real!!!

See Toni Henderson-Mayers bio at the end of her chapter on page 101. Visit her website at www.WiseCourtship.com

Why God Is Real To Me

By Rev. Dr. Tirell A. M. Clifton I, D.Div, M.Div.

People, including some that I know and love, have doubted the existence of God for centuries. I've been baffled by this, because when I take time to ponder life, it never ceases to amaze me that no one seems to be able to come up with a good reason for how life came to exist on this planet. And the only thing that makes sense to me is that an intelligent being made everything come into existence.

I dealt with various situations in which I could have been taken away from life, or my personal freedom could have been denied. Not to mention situations where

God Himself spoke out loud to me, answered unspoken prayers when I was in dire straits, and kept me from serious bodily harm.

When I was younger, in my pre-teens or early teens, I was in my room one day, and my mother was in the living room, sewing. I heard a voice call my name. It said, "Tirell." Thinking that it was my mother, I went into the living room and said, "Yes, ma'am?"
"I didn't call you," she replied, and went back to her sewing, while I went back to my room. I don't remember exactly what I was doing, but I resumed it. Then I heard the voice again. "Tirell." I went back into the living room a second time. "Yes, ma'am?" I said. "I didn't call you." Without missing a beat, my mother continued sewing, and I went back into my room.

About thirty years later, on or around August 17, 2008, I was at work one weekend, doing rounds as a security guard in an apartment complex. Around that time, my second oldest sister, Jerry, had been hospitalized for what would be her final time. The family was preparing for her passage from this life, and she was on my mind and in my thoughts daily. I had just come out of one of the buildings after recording my stop at one of the checkpoints, when a voice out of nowhere spoke to me.

"Jerry does not have much longer left to live." I literally stopped in my tracks. Looking around in just about every direction, I did my best to see where the voice came from. Things like that did not happen to me every day. But the voice was clear, concise, soothing, and non-invasive, as well as unavoidable. I think I was also a little bit frightened by it.

This was two and a half weeks before Jerry succumbed to her illness on September 3. Ever since then, memories of that voice have come back to my remembrance quite often. And at one point over the past nine years or so, it dawned on me that the voice I heard not just in my youth, but that night while I was working, was no one else but Yahweh Elohim. The memory evokes thoughts of young Samuel, when his name was called three times by the Almighty, and he thought that it was Eli calling him.

I consider it unwise to ignore the voice of God when He calls your name. I didn't ignore it that night in 2008, and by not ignoring it, it prompted me to make my way to New Jersey from Baltimore as soon as I could so that I could see my sister one more time before she received the healing from her suffering that she had been praying for years to obtain. Although she did get it on the other side of life, she finally received what she had been asking for.

The sad memory of her face as she lay in the hospital bed, taking her last breaths, comes flooding back and brings tears to my eyes from time to time, but the gratitude that I feel, being able to look into her eyes and let her know that I loved her and that I would see her again, knows no bounds. I may be wrong, but I believe that I was told that she had asked for me before she slipped into what may have been a coma. There was no way that I could not go see my sister after hearing something like that. And shortly after she slipped away, the charge nurse (or at least I believe it was the charge nurse) told me in a private conversation, "She waited for you."

I will never, ever forget that. Hearing that made my grief even worse, but my gratitude even stronger. It let me know that Jerry, who I always knew to be a fighter, held on long enough for my wife and I to make the trip up north so that I would be able to talk to her that final time. While I write this, I have tears in my eyes, and my heart feels as though it wants to burst over like a dam. Just think what may have happened if I had ignored that voice that weekend.

The regret that would have followed me for the rest of my life would have been immeasurable. I probably would never have let myself live that opportunity down if I had lost it by dismissing the voice that I heard loud and clear, as if the person that spoke the words was standing right next to or behind me. I am convinced that a person who doubted the realness of God probably would have just shrugged it off, and blamed it on something else as though it meant nothing, or that his or her imagination was running away with them.

I'm glad that I didn't shrug it off. I believe that it's times like that, in addition to other situations where a need is met even if you never open your mouth and utter a prayer for it to be taken care of, that test the strength of our faith and our belief in a higher power, namely, the God that I was raised to believe and trust in ever since I was four years old. If anything, I feel that it should be proof of His existence, and serve as a reason for an INCREASE in faith,

multiplying it as many times as possible and as necessary.
There's no such thing as luck, and I don't believe in coincidences, because too many of those add up to a plan.

If you believe, then keep on believing. If you trust, then continue to trust. There's a saying that I've seen circulating on the internet over the years…"I would rather live my life as if there is a God and die to find out there isn't, than live as if there isn't and find out that there is."

I'd like to leave you with this…
I'd rather live my life knowing that there is a God and have proof of it every day and die knowing that I will get a chance to finally meet Him, than to live like He doesn't exist and die and be wrong. Peace and blessings.

Rev. Dr. Tirell A. M. Clifton I, D.Div, M.Div.

Tirell Alexander Maxwell "Mack" Clifton I (born April 16, 1969) is a native of Newark, New Jersey who currently resides in Baltimore, Maryland. He is the author of five published books, the owner of First Fruits Publishing, was a Baltimore City mayoral candidate in 2016, and has been an ordained minister for the past seventeen years. He is married to LaWanda, and has children ranging from 28 to 4 years old.

LinkedIn: https://www.linkedin.com/in/tirell-a-m-mack-clifton-i-1bb876110/

God is Real

By Tiffany A. Green

My Story

Who am I, you might ask. I am
Tiffany A. Green. Born and raised
in Chicago. I am 42 years old. I
have two grown children and 3
grandchildren. I totally believe in
Christ Jesus, and I totally believe
that Christ Jesus is God in the
flesh. Because God had to
become flesh in order to be real
on earth and he did it in the
person of Jesus Christ.
I vaguely remember accepting
Christ around 9 or 10 years old. I
didn't know a whole lot about the
Christian Walk and the power of
God. But I did honestly know that I
believed even then that God is
real. At that age I wasn't mature
enough to know what I had tapped
into. It's sad to say but that back

then, around the 80's, I had never been in a church that displayed Gods true power and purpose.

I didn't truly know how real God was until I began to seek my own true relationship. Sometimes we can go through life and not realize what truly matters. From my experiences I can say out of my mouth today that what's number one on my list is knowing God is Real. Now when I say that I'm speaking of his true goodness, I'm speaking of knowing his presence is before you. I'm speaking of spending time with him for hours and experiencing true peace in my spirit.

What brought me to the true knowing that God is Real was watching my mom pray over us daily. Watching her take her Christian walk seriously. And although she died at 53, I have had the pleasure of seeing her prayers come to life. My dad was an alcoholic for years, he is saved and living for Christ today. I was a teenage mom and not sure of who I was I am now walking in my purpose and operating in my gifts God placed in me.

I remember watching Christian television and listening to Creflo Dollar teach on the principles and promises of God. One thing was said about prayer and I starting out praying and spending time with God. I started praying every morning and talking to God.

Before I knew it, my life began to evolve into something I didn't clearly understand, but I knew it was good, it was warm and it was refreshing. I didn't stress over foolishness. I began to think and see things differently.

Even in my failing and making foolish mistakes and how God covered me and protected me in my foolishness. Life doesn't come with instructions and without God I don't know how I would have made it.

Yeah I hear people talk about this self-knowledge stuff, well that's not my story. I say, yes my knowledge came from Christ, my peace comes from Christ, Jesus that is.

In my adult life I look around at how time have changed and I praise God for forgiveness, his mercy and understanding. I view my relationship not as religious or based on religion but based on relationship with Jesus. That's it. That's all. Too many times we forget what matters and what doesn't. I'm mature enough to know that all will not come to him but those who do will experience true everlasting life.

In my prayers I constantly thank God for sending his son to die on the cross for my sins. And always asking for increase in him. Prayer is very delicate and should not be taken lightly or for granted. People are often taught the wrong foundations of prayer. Prayer is simply communicating with the one and true God, Jesus Christ. Communicating is dialogue both ways. We have to listen more than we talk. I've grown to learn that God is so polite that he will not interrupt us while we're talking. So if we're talking he can't say anything. That's why a lot of my prayer has to do with me listening to what he has to say to me. Many people think prayer is about asking for stuff. Naw, in this life I need something more than material things. Peace is what I yearn for from God. Without peace in him I have nothing. God knew we would not be strong enough to live life off of our own understanding. For me the greatest benefit is peace and being able to have faith in him and trust that his word and his Holy Spirit lives in me.

You ask is God Real? He is very real. Now days you hear more conversation about the universe and giving the universe so much credit. My thing is this, who do you think created the universe. God create the universe and all this amazing technology we have. I could never fix my mouth to say man is that intelligent to do all this. After all who created man? God did! Now ask me again is God Real? Yes, he is.

Tiffany A. Green

www.TiffanyTheBrand.com

Only Believe

By Vita Panico

I grew up believing God was real. I was raised in a home where my family believed in God. We attended Catholic church faithfully every single week. My parents had us go through all the sacraments on schedule, which was easy because we attended Catholic schools so we went through the sacraments with all our classmates on a routine schedule.

Even though I pretended to believe in Santa, the Tooth Fairy and the Easter Bunny as long as I could get away with it (so that the presents would keep coming), I did eventually learn that they were not actually real. Even with the realization that I had been misled about these fictional characters my entire life, it still did not put any doubt in my mind about the existence of God. The fact that my parents believed really did shape my beliefs as a child. I definitely questioned God's motives, timing and what felt like His absence in my life sometimes but never His existence.

When I was seven years old my mom gave birth to another little girl. My brother and I were excited to welcome a new tiny sibling into our family but when she was born our family soon learned that she had little chance of survival. She was born with holes in her heart and a missing chromosome. Her name was Christina. When we met her she had a feeding tube in her nose because she was unable to swallow on her own. She cried all the time too and needed all of mom's attention. Despite all her ailments, she was a very active baby. Often she would pull her feeding tube out with her movements and my mom would have to either wait for a nurse to come to the house to put it back in or lug the baby, my little brother and myself with her to the emergency room where we'd wait for hours with a screaming baby for someone to re-insert the tube so my sister could eat. My mom eventually learned to put the tube in herself because she couldn't bear to see the baby cry. When my mom learned to do that the tiny princess started gaining weight and looked almost healthy on the outside. On the inside though, there was still a lot going on and eventually my sister passed away. She was only 7 months old. Our family was devastated.

My parents really struggled for those 7 months of her life and then even more the year after she passed. It was difficult emotionally, physically and spiritually for them. It was hard on my brother and I too but we don't remember a lot about that time, because we were very young. There are some key things that do stand out in my memory though. One of the most significant things I remember is being dragged around a lot to Charismatic Christian healing services. My mom and dad would make us dress up in church clothes and painful dressy shoes and we would always arrive late and the churches would be packed. There was standing room only and the church shoes were unforgiving. The services were long, the preachers would yell, it was always unbearably hot and my brother and I were bored out of our minds. We did not want to be there. However, at the end of each service the preacher would pray for my sister to be healed and we really wanted her to have a miracle. My parents lived for the hope of healing after each of those services. We just went wherever they dragged us next.

Another memory of that season in our lives is that every Sunday my dad would put on a record he had purchased from one of the Evangelists who came to our area, "One day at a time sweet Jesus, that's all I'm asking from you. Just give me the strength to do everything that I have to do. Yesterday's gone sweet Jesus and tomorrow may never be mine. Lord help me today, show me the way, one day at a time.[1]" He would belt it out at the top of his lungs to engage us and unfailingly every time my brother and I would join in the singing. He did this for many years, long after the sting of my sister's passing had subsided.

That season took a hard toll on my dad both spiritually and emotionally. When he speaks about it even to this day, 36 years later, he gets choked up and emotional. He used to work a few hours drive away from home. The day my sister passed, he was on his way home to try to get to the hospital to be with my mom and the baby and at the exact time she passed even though he was still on the road, he says he knew she was gone. Here he was, driving on the highway and he had to pull over to the side of the road because he knew that he knew he had just lost his baby girl and he broke down sobbing on the side of the road.

My parents did not get their miracle healing for their baby girl, but they did not stop believing in God so neither did we. We were left with more questions but my parents didn't have the answers and they still believed so we just followed suit. We continued attending Catholic church faithfully every single week and eventually our broken hearts were repaired. My brother and I were sure of one thing, we were very glad we didn't have to attend those lengthy, loud and uncomfortable church services anymore.

I was bullied by exclusion a lot in both elementary school and high school. I was awkward and out of touch with fashion. I didn't really fit in socially with my peers. I didn't understand why but I also didn't have the self-confidence to ask anyone or enlist a mentor to walk alongside me to help me learn to relate better with my classmates. I coped by pretending I didn't notice when kids didn't invite me to play with them or to their birthday parties. I inserted myself into a group of girls who tolerated me because they were too nice to tell me to leave them alone. When I got the chance to go away with my mom and brother to Italy at the end of eighth grade, instead of being bummed that I would miss my graduation, I was thrilled not to have to go. I did well with my grades in school but I hated every second of elementary school. I often cried myself to sleep at night on school nights because subconsciously I knew I'd have to face another day of being constantly rejected.

My parents had no idea this was going on for me. One of the things that saved me was that I had a lot of cousins and we spent a lot of time with them so my social life at home was healthy. At home I was care-free, happy and content, until bed time. My parents didn't know why I became so "needy" at night.

They would ask me why I was crying and I had no explanation. The truth was, I didn't realize that the sadness and aloneness I was experiencing every night (especially on Sundays) was school related anxiety. I knew the kids didn't like me but I didn't know why and I didn't know how much it was affecting me emotionally. I just counted the minutes until I could run home for lunch and then again until final bell every afternoon.

I should mention that my parents were immigrants to Canada with limited formal education. They didn't understand what school was like for us in Canada. So they wouldn't have thought to connect my emotional distress to my inability to integrate with the other students at school. At home I was social and happy. It was not an easy connection to make. Also, they had just started a garment manufacturing business on a whim which became extremely all-consuming for them. They needed my brother and I to be fine and resilient while they did what they needed to do to keep food on the table with this ambitious new venture; and for the most part we complied.

My parents are both extremely bright and talented and resilient individuals themselves. They were both born in different parts of Italy but met in Toronto. My mom is the oldest of seven siblings and my dad the second youngest of seven siblings. Early in their marriage my father worked as a brick layer and cement finisher for a large crown corporation. My mom stayed home with us kids until we started school, then she worked part time as a seamstress for an upholstery company in Toronto. In Italy she had sown fashion and lingerie and was very skilled at creating patterns and making garments. So when My dad had to be off work for a season because he had severely injured his back on the job an opportunity presented itself and my mom jumped on it. She decided to go into business with her co-worker and open up a sportswear manufacturing business. My dad, realizing that she had no experience as a business owner at all decided to jump in and help them. He didn't have any experience either but that didn't seem to hinder either of them from moving forward.

Shortly thereafter, my mom's partner quit because the stress of running a business was too much for her. My parents grew that little business, from 2 people in a garage to a large operation which employed over 100 people at its peak. Not bad for two minimally educated immigrants from agricultural backgrounds, right?

You might be wondering what all of this has to do with whether or not God is real. I'm about to get into that. You see, destinies are not haphazard. They are carefully cultivated and orchestrated by God, with our cooperation, even when we do not even know we are cooperating with Him. He is the master craftsman who shapes our futures as they unfold and he allows for multiple routes to account for our free will with the goal that they will all lead to a place where we cross our own fulfilling finish lines.

When I started high school in grade nine I made a friendship that eventually changed my life forever. I had business class for homeroom on the first day of grade nine (freshman year). Needless to say that given my insecurities and awkward appearance I was terrified of high school. In that first class, the only person I knew was a girl I went to elementary school with. She was one of the girls who tolerated me in eighth grade so it gave me some comfort to see her in my class. We actually had known each other since second grade but had never become friends. In that class though we were assigned to work on a project together and she discovered for the first time that I was actually funny and smart and kind and friendly and she really enjoyed my company. She made a decision in a moment that changed the trajectory of my life. Despite any social stigma she would encounter for hanging out with me, she determined that she was my friend and told me so. That is a huge decision in high school where reputation matters more than academics sometimes. Her selfless act made high school mostly bearable although I did skip class a lot to study and work at home or in the library. We are still best friends to this day.

I'd love to tell you that with her help and influence I finished high school on the higher end of the social rankings but that would be a lie. I was as unpopular in grade twelve as I was in grade nine. However, with her help, I did meet a great group of girlfriends who meant the world to me and helped me grow socially during that four year period. The miracle happened during the summer between Junior and Senior year (grades eleven and twelve). At the end of eleventh grade I had a bit of a meltdown while I was at home alone. I was crying and hurting about an incident that happened at school and I looked up to the ceiling of our second floor hallway with my face towards heaven and yelled up to God, "Why don't they like me?" Then I went to the bathroom mirror, looked at myself and said, "I'm not ugly. I'm not cruel. I'm not that bad. Why don't they like me?" I got no response from God of course, I didn't really expect to. I did say to myself in that same mirror, "they don't like you because you do weird things like this." I dried my eyes and tried to forget what I had just done.

That incident was unforgettable though because although I didn't realize it, it did two critical things for me. First, it was the first time I had looked myself in the eye and said out loud, "I'm not ugly." I believed I was ugly up until that point, but that day I realized that I was not ugly. I didn't think I was drop dead gorgeous after that, but it was huge for me to hear myself say, "I'm not ugly." The second thing it did was prepare me for the miracle that was going to happen later that summer.

My best friend shared some news with me before the end of eleventh grade (junior year) that she would be going away for the entire summer to Portugal with her family. I was happy for her but mortified for me. I had visions of summer hang-outs and all kinds of fun plans for summer break but they all came crashing down with her announcement. I still had a lovely summer with cousins and other friends but I missed her a lot. When she came home, we were on the phone for hours as she recounted all the details of her fabulous adventures overseas. At one point she told me about an argument she had had with someone there and as she was explaining it to me she said something that became a key for my life path from that point forward. The words she said were, "I sat on my bed and I was talking to God and God said…," and I didn't hear anything she said after that. I didn't know what to think but I definitely needed an explanation. I told her to stop and rewind the conversation. She didn't understand what I meant at first but I explained to her, "hello … you said God said! Are you trying to tell me God talks to you?" Part of me thought my friend had lost her mind and part of me wanted to believe her so badly that it hurt. I remembered my conversation with God that day in my upstairs hallway and wondered if the words, "I am not ugly," came from Him. No one had ever said God would or could talk to me before, not even the priests on Sunday mornings. I knew, because I listened intently every Sunday in church searching for nuggets of truth that would speak to my heart. She told me it was true, that God really did speak to her and give her an answer for her dilemma. I asked her why God didn't speak to me and she told me I had to accept Jesus into my heart first, confess that He is my Lord and Saviour, ask Him to forgive all my sins and believe that He would come and live on the inside of me and be the Lord of my life. So I did. Then I began to wait for God to speak to my heart every time I prayed. He always came. Sometimes I would see visions and sometimes He would tell me He loves me. He never disappointed me though.

My friend had just recently prayed that prayer herself so we went on a journey of faith together, growing in God. We found out that her

Catholic priest had healing masses during the week and her mom needed a healing miracle, so she invited me to come with them. At that service the Catholic priest was speaking in tongues (a biblical language) and he was putting his hands on people and they were falling down as he prayed for them. My friend asked me if I was "freaked out" but I wasn't because it was no different than what I had experienced as a child in those Charismatic Pentecostal Healing Services. It felt safe and familiar to me.

Soon I started attending that Catholic church instead of the one I grew up in because I felt like this priest could lead us to better understanding of what it means to know God. I convinced my family to join me. They did reluctantly. However, on Sunday, the priest didn't speak in tongues or lay hands on anyone or teach us how He did that or how we could grow in our personal relationship with God.

Soon, my friend and I needed to find a church that could help answer some of our questions about God and faith. We were looking for a spiritual coach or a mentor (even though we would not have put it in those terms at the time). There was so much we didn't understand and we were hungry to tap in to more of God. We lived only thirty minutes away from the Toronto Airport Vineyard Church (now called Catch the Fire Toronto) where a revival had broken out. We didn't know what a revival was but we went to check it out and found ourselves hit by the power of God and laughing so hard we fell to the ground and could not get back up. We felt electricity flowing through our bodies like we had never experienced and could not control our bodies from shaking. For all of you skeptics out there, please note, there was no Kool-Aid anywhere in sight. We felt like we were out of our minds but looked around and everyone else was going through similar manifestations of God's power and glory. The thing is, we were out of our minds, we were in the spirit and we knew it. We liked it. God was awesome and loving and kind and He wanted to connect on a deep personal level with us. He wanted to shake us out of our rigid conformity and teach us to surrender to Him.

Then one night we went to a woman's meeting near our home and experienced that same "presence" of God that we did at the revival but coupled with teaching that made things so clear that we understood it. Not only did we understand it but we received prophetic prayer answers to things only God knew we needed. We discovered that we could hear his voice through the word of God. We started going to this women's group once a month and then eventually decided to check out the church on Sunday mornings. Twenty-four years later and I am still attending that same church today.

Over the years my brother and I have taken over and transformed my parent's business which has been my brother's brainchild and passion. Mine has been personal growth and helping people find breakthrough. Our journeys have been different but faith has been an anchor. Our parent's fearlessness and willingness to step into the unknown has been a

model for us on how to launch out
into our dreams.

I truly believe that there are no
such things as co-incidences.
Every step we take becomes the
catalyst and launching pad for the
next step in our journey. God is in
the little things. He lives in the still
small voice and the hunches and
gut-feelings. You have had them
and acted on them without even
recognizing it was Him. I'm sure of
it. He nudges us along and longs
for us to hit that place of purpose
and fulfilment He wants us to
have. God is present, the question
is, are we giving Him the space He
needs to reveal Himself to us. Are
we surrendering to His nudges so
that we move forward along the
path of our destiny assignments?

I have learned a lot over the years
in my faith journey but nothing
more powerful than this, God is

always speaking, it is our job to get ourselves on the right frequency to hear His voice. We hear Him through the word when it is taught and when we read it ourselves. If you want to know Him, read His word. It is alive. We hear Him through others when they are teaching and when they are prophesying. I have had several prophetic words which resonate deeply with me over the years. The reason they resonate so deeply is because God and I had already had the conversations before the prophet gave me the word. Prophets will often come and confirm a word that God has already whispered in your heart, that's why it resonates with us. It has to be a God-thing or else how could they know? I have had a prophet come to minister at our church from a Mid-Western state in the United States who, having never met me, proceed to tell me the same message God spoke to me in a private journaling moment while I was away for a personal development retreat in California three years prior to the prophet's arrival. Also, no one could have known that just that week I had been asking God if that promise was still true even three years later. God sent the prophet to strengthen my faith in the waiting. Today I am walking in a season of the realization of that word and it is exciting.

Is God real? He is to me. No one can tell me He isn't because I have experienced Him for myself. The bible says, "Taste and see that the Lord is good."[2] I can't taste something using someone else's taste buds. I need to use my own. Each of us must have our own real experiences with God. That is what is missing in this generation. We've been programmed to only look for the supernatural in dark places instead of seeing and experiencing it in the safety of God's loving arms.

When you look for God, you will find Him because He loves to be found. He loves to reward those who diligently seek Him. There is a caveat though, you must suspend your disbelief while you search. Trust me, you can choose faith. The scripture says, "And without faith living within us it would be impossible to please God. For we come to God in faith knowing that he is real and that he rewards the faith of those who give all their passion and strength into seeking him."[3] We have to approach God with the assumption that He is real, because faith is our currency to activate the supernatural.

With my Italian background, I've heard stories of relatives who practiced a counter spell to the curse of the evil eye (Malocchio). I myself have never practiced it or asked anyone to practice it on me. However, there are many who believe it works. There are many who believe it is harmless superstition. I don't doubt that they are tapping in to the supernatural and I wouldn't call it harmless at all. It isn't God's power they are accessing. There are good and bad spirits all around us, we must be aware of what we dabble in. When we use the power of a spirit that is not of God to protect us from "evil," it is my belief that we are walking in to a trap. My question to you is, why is it easier to believe in breaking curses by a ritual than it is to believe God wants to speak with you personally every single day. Who would you like to put your faith in?

I choose Jesus, the one who laid His own life down so that I could live in victory. I choose Jesus who protects me from the curse before it even lands. I choose Jesus whose love and light is available to all if we will only believe.

I think that part of the disconnect we have today as a society is that we live average lives with no expectation that the supernatural realm is real and we are ok with that. This is sad because we were never meant to live average lives. The moment we say yes to Jesus, ask Him to come into our heart, forgive our sins and be Lord of our lives, if we believe it, we automatically have access to the supernatural realm in Christ.

If you want to have an encounter with the one true living God, I encourage you to pray the prayer that I prayed in high school with faith in your heart that He will meet you. He is more excited to welcome you with open arms than you are to discover He is real. Pray this prayer:

Dear Jesus, I confess that I am a sinner in need of a saviour. I ask you today to forgive me of all my sin. I invite you to come into my life and make my heart your personal residence. Lead me and guide me and be both the saviour of my soul and the lord of my life. I believe you are real, please show me your glory. In Jesus' name … Amen.

If you want to learn more about how to grow in your faith, please feel free to connect with me at vitapanico.com or Vita Panico on all social platforms. I would love to hear about your journey of faith and help you discover that not only is God real, He has a plan for your life and it's a good one! I promise.

1. Lyrics to "One Day at a Time." Genius, May 30, 2018, https://genius.com/Cristy-lane-one-day-at-a-time-lyrics
2. Ps. 34:8 (New International Version) - from biblegateway.com, March 30, 2018, https://www.biblegateway.com/passage/?search=Ps.+34%3A8&version=NIV
3. Heb. 11:6 (The Passion Translation) - from biblegateway.com, March 30, 2018, https://www.biblegateway.com/passage/?search=Hebrews%2011:5-7&version=TPT

Vita Panico

is a lover of Jesus, a church leader, a mentor and a coach-by-nature (before life-coaching was a thing). She always sees the good and the potential in everyone and it is her desire to help all of those in her sphere of influence to find their God-ordained purpose and live with passion. Vita leads the corporate and intercessory prayer ministry at her church and thrives on seeing people tap in to the gifts of God available to them by faith. She is the creator of This Proverbial Life a 31-day bible study that will ignite your passion for the word and reset your relationship with God. Vita is also the author of the soon to be released book The Gatekeeper, a book which will help individuals discover which sphere of influence they belong in and help them find the gate they were meant to man. Jesus said "upon this rock I will build my church and the gates of hell will not prevail against it." It is time the body of Christ discovers their position and stands firmly in place giving no way to the enemy who is attempting to gain access illegally. He has already been defeated, you have the victory. The book is available now for pre-order on Vita's website vitapanico.com. You can find her on socials by going to www.facebook.com/vitapanico2 or search Vita Panico on IG, Twitter and Snapchat.

A Soldier's Testimony

By Rev. Andrew Payne, M.Div

I was raised by my grandparents in a small coal mining community in rural West Virginia. My family attended Bethel Missionary Baptist Church in Cannelton, West Virginia. As a child there was nothing more exciting than going to church. Although I thoroughly enjoyed Sunday school, my favorite part of any church services that I attended was devotions. Devotions were conducted by two deacons that led the congregation in prayer, testimonies and congregational hymns of praise to God.

Typically, after the deacons would pray devotional service would be opened to congregational testimonies and hymns. After an earnest testimony a hymn of praise would be sung out of "The National Baptist Hymnal". Frankly, I cannot remember if the hymn would be sung before or after the testimony but I do remember that often the hymns were being sung with fervor and zeal. Even though I could feel Gods presence and was sympathetic when the elder saints would sing songs and hymns of praise I was not empathetic. Yes, I could definitely feel and share the presence of the Holy Ghost when they sang hymns of praise but I could not understand why they sang with such excitation.

The absence of empathy for the ardor of the saints was due to the dearth of my own life experiences. Simply, what the elder saints had sang about with fervor, zeal and passion through hymnals were testimonies of their life's experiences and supported their spoken devotional testimonies that, "Yes, God Is Real". Most of the churches in those coal communities are abandoned or closed, those old saints have all passed away and now I have my own testimony and hymn of praise that, "Yes, God is Real". Now I can sympathize and empathize with those saints and I share these testimonies with you.

I did two tours of duty in the US Army as a Chaplain Assistant Camp Anaconda in Ballad Iraq durning OIF2 and OIF 6-8. During OIF2 we experienced twenty to thirty mortars and or rocket attacks from insurgents daily. These mortars and rockets were known to cause mass casualties by exploding on impact and destroying whatever they hit; such as, military buildings, housing, vehicles, equipment and personnel. Upon impact they would often disseminate hot led or steel that was razor sharp and could easily pierce the kevlar body armor of soldiers and cause serious injury or death. As a matter of fact, the impact of the rockets and mortars alone could transform rocks and gravel into propelled projectiles with so much force that they were capable of putting softball size holes in hard buildings (cement). Needless to say that these projectiles had the potential to cause serious injury or death and were capable of penetrating through vehicles and trailers used as office space and sleeping quarters.

Accompanying these rocket and mortar attacks were loud earth rattling and core shaking booms that would leave your very soul startled and in pain. The sheer impact and force of the explosions were numbing, dazing and felt as if someone was jumping on your internal organs with spiked cleats.

It was numerous daily assaults by insurgents through mortar and rocket fire that taught me that "Yes God is real". For instance, the insurgents were infamous for their poor aim when attacking our post. However, they were persistent and becoming more accurate with time. One early evening after duty myself and three other soldiers were standing outside of our sleeping quarters talking. Suddenly, we heard a loud roar over our heads that we all thought was an air force jet flying low. During a quick glance up we noticed a faint smoke trail above our heads. Instantly the E-4 that was facing the direction of what we all thought was a jet exclaimed, "That wasn't no jet.

That was a rocket." Almost instantaneously there was an earth shaking and teeth rattle explosion that blew up the DEFAC (cafeteria) near our quarters.

In a prior instance, a rocket pierced through the ceiling, went through the floor and stuck in the sand under one of the trailers in our sleeping quarters without detonating. Fortunately, there were no casualties and most of the soldiers were at work including the soldiers that was assigned that trailer. Because of the day's events that night I felt the spiritual urgency through an unction of the Holy Spirit to privately pray over and anoint the doors of our quarters. I accomplished this by simply drawing a cross on the center of doors and praying sincerely for the safety and protection of every soldier in every room whether they were believers or not. Then the Holy Spirit urged me to pray for the entire housing area and then honored the prayer by the mortars ceasing in that particular housing area.

In another instance a contracted civilian employee that worked in the DFAC for the United States Government in OIF2 witnessed to me about the goodness of God one afternoon. He said the incident took place early one morning while preparing to go work. He woke up, got dressed for work and was standing outside of his sleeping quarters. Suddenly he could hear what sounded like a mortar falling out of the sky. Immediately he crouched and grabbed his knees as quickly as he could. He then heard a loud earth shattering explosion. After the blast he stood up stunned and amazed that he had survived. He gave me his testimony of how God spared him.

On another occasion in OIF2 one of the group of young reserve soldiers that was attached to the 13th COSCOM in Fort Hood Texas with me had fallen on concertina wire. She was a very hard working and motivated soldiers of Hispanic descent. She came to me concerned and explaining what had happened while simultaneously showing me her hands. Both of her hands had several very fine small cuts in the palms but were not bleeding as of yet. I held her hands and began to pray in Jesus names for my little sister's health and healing and told her to go to the infirmary. A week later I inquired about the progress of her hands and with a smile on her face she showed me the palms of her hands. They looked as if nothing had happened. I stood in amazement of what God did.

In another occurrence on Camp Anaconda in OIF2 frequently the Chaplain gave vehicle access to the chaplain assistants to go to lunch and run errands. There were a variety of DFACS on camp Anaconda and I attempted to eat at each of them before my tour of duty was over. On this particular day one of my battle buddies and I had decided to go to the civilian contractor DFAC. While on the way we passed the Army Air Force Exchange Service (PX). The PX is the retailer on U. S. Army and Air Force installations worldwide. My battle buddy and passenger explained that something was telling him that we should go to the PX and hang out for lunch. I disagreed and explained that whatever he heard I did not hear and that we were going to the civilian DFAC to eat. When we arrived at the DFAC we took our kevlar vest and head gear (battle rattle) off and kept our weapons by our sides.

As soon as we got our food and began to eat we could feel the continual pounding of mortars exploding in the nearby vicinity. The civilians began putting on their protective gear and scurrying out to the bunkers. The food was good, we were tired and decided not to leave but to finish our food while discretely chuckling at the civilians. Suddenly, out of nowhere a small elderly white haired gentleman of Anglo Saxon ancestry stood in front of us and admonished us by asking that we put our battle rattle back on. We agreed in hopes that he would go away so that we could finish our food in peace and then quickly leave.

He turned around again with his hands clasped behind his back and kindly made his requested again. He was dressed in a tan military style uniform with a colonel insignia on his chest. We immediately complied by putting on our protective gear, throwing away our trash and following him out of the door. The gentleman was in arm's length in front of us while we were exiting the DFAC and suddenly he disappeared right before our eyes. While returning to our areas of operations we drove past the PX that my battle buddy wanted to spend lunch at earlier and discover it had been decimated by a mortar attacks. We could see the civilians and soldiers alike assisting each other while exiting the exchange covered in dust. We both began to thank God for steering us away from the PX for lunch and allowing us to entertain an angel unaware (Hebrews 13:2) in the elderly gentleman at the civilian DFAC.

My final experience was on my first tower guard duty on Camp Anaconda. Anaconda was approximately 44 to 50 miles long and had numerous towers along the perimeter for protection. It was a beautiful afternoon that was quiet and peaceful. Myself and my battle buddy from Trinidad were pulling guard duty in a seventy-five-foot-high steel tower. We were making our hourly radio checks when suddenly we heard a thunderous thud and saw a puff of smoke inside the perimeter 25 yards to our immediate left. What it appeared to be was a mortar that did not explode. While trying to report the incident through radio communications we were immediately interrupted by towers 33 or 34 that were on the other side of Anaconda. They were reporting attacks by insurgents and were requesting QRF support when suddenly headquarters ordered them to change to a more secure radio channel. After my first shift of tower guard was over I had become extremely concerned that the insurgent would attack our tower during our final shift.

That evening when we returned for the final tower guard duty I had been preparing myself by praying for the Lord's protection. I requested that if the insurgents were to attack us that I would destroy the enemy or die honorably trying. I did not want my family to see my dead carcass being defiled and drug through the streets of Iraq on CNN. For this reason, I was extra attentive and observant while on tower guard. While doing a constant check of my perimeter I noticed a small black speck in the clouds that was growing by the minute. Seemingly in seconds the black speck had become a full storm. The clouds were as black as suit with highlights of gray entangled in the them. Lightning filled the sky and thunder rumbled so strongly that it the shook the ground. It shook so forcefully I thought the ground would crack and swallow the tower. It was at this time I saw just how big and powerful God is and how insignificant, powerless and small I am compared to Him.

The storm was low and the tower was high and it felt as if the storm was just above my head and in my grasp. Then it began to rain in buckets and it felt as if wherever I turned my head a fire hose of water was sprayed in my face. As

I reached for my chair to sit in I realized that my battled buddy had my chair over his head to shield himself from the rain. The wind and water was so forceful that the water began to run down my shirt and filled my boots. At that time I cried to God and reminded Him that I was in a 75 foot high steel tower in the worst storm I had ever experienced, I was wet and lighting was striking all around and He promised me that nothing would happen to me on this deployment while convoying across IRAQ to get to Camp Anaconda. Then I heard His voice so clear so calm reminding me that the enemy could not attack with rocket or mortar in this kind of weather. I had Gods assurance, peace and joy that I was safe in the storm.

Like the old saints that I grew up around in Rural West Virginia I can testify that through my life experiences and struggles I know for myself that "Yes God is real." I have seen and felt his healing power. God had kept his angels around me to protect from all hurt, harm and danger. He heard my cry and honored my plea for His protection. I have seen his power. Without a doubt I can Say, "Yes, God is Real". The great song writer Kenneth Morrison explains like this, *"There are some things, I may not know, There are some places, I can't go, But I'm sure, Of this one thing, That God is real, For I can feel, Him deep within, Yes, God is real, Real in my soul, Yes, God is real, For He has washed, And made me whole, His love for me, Is like pure gold, Yes, God is real, For I can feel, Him in my soul".*

Rev. Andrew T. Payne

has a Masters of Divinity from Shaw Divinity in Raleigh NC and is currently the Director of Christian Education at Providence Baptist Church in Rockingham NC. He served two tours of duty in Ballad Iraq as a Chaplain Assistant.

Yes, God Is Real

By LeRoy A. Smith

Yes, I am a church-baby.

I was 'born and raised' in the church to the fullest extent of the phrase. My family *always* went to church; even on vacations. I can confidently say that I know "church"; I know what to do and when, where and how to do it.

I can sing, I can play, preside and usher. I know how to serve communion, quote scriptures and receive offerings. I know how to look, talk and act. I know how to enhance and magnify the emotional feelings and moods of a church service.

I pretty much know all of the ins and outs of the business and the behind-the-scenes operations of church. Even without having the proper credentials, I probably could conduct a wedding, give a good eulogy or write a pretty decent sermon.

All of that is great but the question I am being asked is "how do I know that God is real"?

> "I can feel Him in my hands
> I can feel Him in my feet
> I can feel Him all over me!"

Seriously? There really should be a simple answer to this, especially from someone like myself.

The good thing about being 'raised' in the church, is knowing *how* to 'church'.

The flipside is that the actions and behaviors associated with this can sometimes become too common. I find that I can do it so much and so often that, if I'm not careful, it can all become more ritualistic than realistic.

I do recognize that God is way more than my physical senses or my finite mind can comprehend or articulate.

The heavens declare the glory of God, and the expanse proclaims the work of his hands. Psalms 19:1

Since the earliest recognition of time, people have questioned if God exists.

It would seem that most people believe in God in one form or another. Throughout the world, assemblies of every nationality gather, perform rituals and ceremonies because we all 'believe' that there is a God, some 'higher power' that is greater than us all.

Most of the world's situations and conditions exist because of different individuals' beliefs in God. Many wonderful things have been experienced as well as some of history's most horrific events have occurred over how people believe that they should best serve Him.

The earth is the LORD's and the fullness thereof, the world and those who dwell therein, Psalms 24:1

I believe God is real because of the many wonders of this world, the complexity of creation, the vastness of the universe, and the details of the earth that I share with every living thing on it.

I marvel at God's handiwork and am constantly amazed at how much He cares for EVERYTHING. There is not one thing, not one single detail of creation that God is not aware of. Every blade of grass, every drop of water, each grain of sand, every single insect, animal, bird or sea creature, everything we see and cannot see is known by Him and even with all of that going on, He still is able to see me and everything I am, everything I experience and feel.

Give all your worries and cares to God, for he cares about you. I Peter 5:7

I believe that God is real because I sense that He cares about me.

It is often assumed that I have everything together, that every aspect of my life is in order, because of my church and religious background, while the truth is that I'm often a mess.

I have learned through His care that God is a forgiver. I know that my life should have ended so many times and so many years ago because of my unfaithfulness to Him. He has been faithful and just to forgive me of things that I will probably never mention.

I have come to understand that God has been my protector. I have had several accidents; I have even been hit by a car. I've been in the wrong place at the wrong time where bullets have flown past me. I've had a gun held to my head more times than I wish to even count. In spite of myself, I am alive today and I know that it is not because I have been good all of the time, but I know it has been His mercy and kindness to me.

God is my provider. I have been without money. I've been without possessions. I've been in situations where I didn't know how my family and I would make it. But, I have never been without my needs met at the time I needed them. I've never been without a place to stay.

God is my comforter. I've experienced bouts of deep depression to the point of wanting to give up because I believed in the momentary appearances of my life situations more than I believed in Him. But, again in spite of myself, I have found comfort in God as I have had to learn to continually TRUST Him.

Trust in the LORD with all your heart; do not depend on your own understanding. Seek his will in all you do, and he will show you which path to take. Proverbs 3:5-6

It is through my many life experiences that I continue to understand the realness of God. Through good and bad, joy and pain, hope and sorrow, I get to 'see' and know God more and more.

From seeing the birth of my children and witnessing the death or rather the transitioning of my father, my heart and mind have been overwhelmed with so many different feelings that are sometimes so far away from the next, that I am not able to describe them.

I know that God has been with me through every single experience, even though I often was too involved in them to notice Him at the time.

My father's illness and death really tried my faith in God. I greatly struggled with it all.

I knew God was real in all of it, but sometimes I felt like He was being distant, unfair and too slow to act. I knew He cared about my Dad because he had served Him for so many years, but I wondered if He cared about how those times made 'us' feel.

It was hard to see my father go from physically being the strongest person I knew to a point of physical weakness where he required the help of others. As it became more obvious that my Dad's time on earth was coming to an end, I became comforted in God by my father's faith in God and how much Dad wanted to be with his Lord.

My Dad would sometimes get mad when he would wake up and find that he had not gone to be with God. I couldn't understand it. It seemed a little crazy at first, but I soon began to realize that this is what faith in God is. To be able to put everything in His hands, no matter what things may look like and let it go and trust Him.

Strange as it may sound, it was watching my Dad take his last breath and leaving us to go to the God he believed and trusted in; that increased my faith. It caused me to seek God in a deeper, more personal and sincerer way.

It caused me to remember that no matter what I go through, no matter how tough life gets and no matter how much hurt and pain I feel, and yes, this was PAINFUL, that God is there to carry me through everything.

It is through my every life experience that I get the opportunity to learn God more. Some days it takes me longer to 'get' the lesson than others, but I am starting to get it.

I know that God is real. Not because I've been in church ALL of my life, but because I know and am still learning that He has been with me, ALL of my life.

LeRoy A. Smith

nucreationmusic@gmail.com

LeRoy A. Smith of NuCreation Music, is a New Jersey native, a songwriter, writer, singer and musician.

LeRoy is one of the contributing songwriters for *Beyond The Silence*, an independent movie by William Michael Barbee of Prestige Media.

LeRoy is currently the Music Director for Kingdom Work Productions, a New Jersey based theater group. With KWP, he has worked on the stage-play, *Marriage, the Musical* and is the producer of the play's sound track. He has

91

also been featured in other KWP stage plays, *The Order of Love*, *From Chains To Change* and *Measure Of A Man* in which he performs his original song *Be A Man*.

LeRoy has done musical work for the stage plays, *Soul Of A Man* and *The Morning After* and is currently working as the sound engineer for A'ndre Davis', *Man Of The House*.

LeRoy is the Minister Of Music at the St. Luke AME Church of Newark and also serves in the music ministry at Union Gospel Tabernacle, of Newark.

LeRoy has served as a musician at Beulah Gospel Tabernacle UHC, in Bayonne, the First Baptist Church of Woodbridge, Mt. Zion House of Prayer UHC, in Red Bank, and Greater Mt. Moriah Baptist Church in Linden.

He has also sung and played for the North New Jersey District YPHA choir, North New Jersey Concert Chorale and the United Holy Church's General and Northern District's Mass choirs.

LeRoy has written and played for the bands Redeemed, M-Prov and Elect Of God, each providing music for many diverse events including worship services, weddings, banquets, golf outings, community and political functions.

LeRoy is a proud graduate of Arts High School in Newark, NJ, and has continued his education at New Jersey City University, Gibbs College, the Groove Academy in Edison, NJ and the United Christian College in Roselle, NJ.

LeRoy, his wife Audrey and their three children happily reside together in New Jersey.

Aunt Bessie

By Toni Henderson-Mayers, MA, MA, MBA

There are so many stories I could share, so many instances where God has made himself real to me. Like others who have shared in this book, I have been with the Lord a very long time. My Dad, the late Rev. Dr. Steve C. Henderson, Jr. was a prolific Pastor and preacher, my Mom, Alma J. Henderson, long time Christian who once wanted to live her life as a missionary before getting married and starting a family were major influencers in my life. Their commitment and love to God was evident, not only in the speaking, preaching and teaching but in the private moments of their lives. I was impressed even as a child of their ability to be the same "behind the scenes", if you will, as they were in the public eye. They loved God and God's people and they dedicated their lives to serving others even without much money, recognition or accolades.

For some their belief in God stems from their childhood and never becomes a personal relationship between them and God only. In other words, many believe simply because their parents or grandparents did and that is good for them. However, this is not my story. At some point in life whether one is raised in the church or not, you have to address the question of whether God is real.

My answers came early for me in my life as a child as I endured seven long years of the most malicious and cruel bullying by children and adults. As a matter of fact, I accepted Jesus as my Lord and Savior at the age of seven; the very onset of this abuse after hearing a visiting preacher say, "God loves us, just the way we are." That message resonated with me and blesses me even after all these years. It helped me get through seven years of abuse of haters, lies and mistreatment.

I could reflect on the times, God called my name in the night, how he healed my body, stood up for me in the midst of persecution and false accusations, near death experiences, financial calamity, death of loved ones, depression, thoughts of suicide and so much more. However, instead of pulling from the many times God has shown himself strong in my life, I want to tell you about a time that God delivered someone else and how it reaffirmed his existence to me.

I want to share this example because after reading this book, you may feel God can only speak directly to you (and he can) or can only call your name audibly (and he can) or do something spectacular for you only (and he can). God can also work miracles for others and simply by you watching or being in the surrounding area, that situation just witnessed can speak to your heart as well. God can speak and make himself real to all of us at the same time.

In one particular example, a woman who was kind to me as a child became like a second Mom to me. I called her my "Aunt Bessie". One day after a wedding Aunt Bessie fell ill and blacked out. She had a stroke. Initially the doctors said she would not survive and they called for the family members to come to the hospital to say their final goodbyes. I arrived with my Mom and there was Aunt Bessie with tubes connected seemingly all over her body. She was breathing hard and her breath had a queer rattle to it as she exhaled. My Mom referred to it as a "Death Rattle". This term, "Death Rattle" was a term she heard her people use and it depicted a form of breathing that precluded someone's death. The African American ancestry is a unique one in that although we were forced to operate with limited resources we developed an uncanny ability to discern moments in our lives, develop our own medical treatments, and a host of other things I don't have time to get into right now.

With the knowledge of the severity of Aunt Bessie's situation, we all clasped hands and began to pray. Prayer has always and still is our connection with God. It is simply talking to him and asking him for his guidance, wisdom or intervention.

Once the prayer was done, there was no immediate change. We just comforted one another and began to go home. By the time we got home, we received a telephone call. The caller said the doctor wasn't sure what happened, but Aunt Bessie's condition had made a turn for the better! Praise God!!! What a miracle! We were so excited!!!!

While we were celebrating, the caller continued to say, the doctor said but……Aunt Bessie will be a vegetable. Her brain suffered too much damage. She won't have a quality life. I wonder has anyone been in a similar situation where you go from a low place to a high place only to be brought back low again? We had only about 10 seconds of amazing happiness, 10 seconds to praise God for his goodness, 10 seconds to enjoy what he did for Aunt Bessie only to be brought back down to that awful low place. What do you do, when you're brought back to a low place? You pray and believe God.

Once again we all gathered to pray; the family, church, neighbors and friends. After praying, a few days later, Aunt Bessie began to show signs of brain activity and intelligence. We were elated! However, after Aunt Bessie received several tests, the doctor said she will not be able to talk or walk again.

Of course he was proved wrong as we began to address her being able to talk and walk in our prayers. I learned quickly that one needs to be specific with their prayers and pray above all believing. Aunt Bessie began to talk and walk some, but I noticed something was very wrong!

In my conversations with Aunt Bessie, it was apparent she was addressing me as a little girl and not a young woman. Not only that, she thought my father was alive and he had been deceased for a few years prior. In addition, Aunt Bessie was a mild mannered woman, joyful and patient. She seemed to be "matter of fact" like, impatient and not as joyful. After the doctor tested Aunt Bessie, he said that her mentality, her mind, would remain that way for the rest of her life. You would think the doctor would have learned a little about the power of prayer by now, but he didn't. (smile)

We prayed yet again for Aunt Bessie and you guessed it over

time she gained all her memory, mental ability, speech, ability to walk and all else that was damaged by her stroke. She was healed 100% and it was all by the hand of God Almighty! She made a full recovery. Her situation spoke to all of us that God does exist and that he cares about our situation. The doctors and staff reaffirmed their faith and some believed in God for the first time. The staff knew that Aunt Bessie's recovery was at the hand of God because all along the way they had given her up and God proved them all wrong.

God is a sovereign God which means he decides when and what to do what he wants to do. In this instance he healed Aunt Bessie, possibly because of the many people who needed to know of his existence. I cannot pretend to know why God heals some and allows others to die, but I do know that he has his reasons and all works out well whether we can see or understand it.

When God does not answer our prayer the way we think he should, it does not mean he is not working on our behalf. He works on a greater scale with a greater plan than we can imagine. My sons didn't always understand why I didn't let them eat cookies for breakfast, lunch and dinner. I knew that they needed vegetables and other nutrients to make them strong and develop. My wisdom is something they could not understand at the time, but was working for their good. God who is a much better Father than I am a Mother, works for our better good. His answers are yes and amen. Whether his answer is yes, no or wait, it will be better than we expected. We may not understand it in this life always but definitely in the life to come.

God is real. He has shown himself strong in my life and the lives of so many others. The stories you have read in this book are actual accounts of God's presence. Toward the end of Vita's chapter around page 55, she tells you how to receive Jesus into your heart so you too can begin a relationship with God. I highly recommend you do so.

Once you pray the prayer of salvation (receive Jesus in your heart, see page 55), then pray this prayer: "God reveal yourself to me." He will come to you and bless you. He wants a relationship with you. He will make himself real to you too!

Toni Henderson-Mayers

is the author of, "One Great Idea", which is collaboration with other successful business colleagues on various business ideas. *Her book, "Wise Courtship: Before Relationship & Marriage Guide" has earned worldwide distribution and audience and a nomination for a Shelf Award and finalist for an Indie Author Legacy Award.* She is also a contributing writer to the book, "Share & Grow Rich" and "Hiring Now" Magazine. **Toni is the winner of the People Choice Award with ACHI Magazine**, radio show is on a Stellar Award winning station and LIVE TV show, Never Settle Show won an Emmy where she served as Crowd Producer.

Toni is married to actor and playwright Brian McClure and has two sons and travels to speak, perform and make TV and radio appearances. Visit her on her website at www.WiseCourtship.com

Appendix

WISE COURTSHIP

Before Relationship & Marriage Guide

Toni Henderson-Mayers

Foreword by Cora Jakes-Coleman, Potter's House, Dallas, TX

Order your copy of this award winning book from an award winning author at
www.WiseCourtship.com

Order this amazing anthology by
Toni Henderson-Mayers at
www.WordTherapyPublishing.com

We publish messages that heal.

word♥therapy
P U B L I S H I N G™

www.WordTherapyPublishing.com